W9-BZL-754

PARTICIPANT'S
GUIDE

FORENSIC
FAITH

PARTICIPANT'S
GUIDE

FORENSIC
FAITH

A Homicide Detective Makes the Case for a
More Reasonable, Evidential Christian Faith

J. WARNER WALLACE

David C Cook®
transforming lives together

FORENSIC FAITH PARTICIPANT'S GUIDE
Published by David C Cook
4050 Lee Vance Drive
Colorado Springs, CO 80918 U.S.A.

David C Cook U.K., Kingsway Communications
Eastbourne, East Sussex BN23 6NT, England

The graphic circle C logo is a registered trademark of David C Cook.

All rights reserved. Except for brief excerpts for review purposes,
no part of this book may be reproduced or used in any form
without written permission from the publisher.

The website addresses recommended throughout this book are offered as a resource
to you. These websites are not intended in any way to be or imply an endorsement
on the part of David C Cook, nor do we vouch for their content.

Unless otherwise noted, all Scripture quotations are taken from the New American Standard Bible®, copyright
© 1960, 1995 by The Lockman Foundation. Used by permission. (www.Lockman.org.) Scripture quotations
marked ESV are taken from the ESV® Bible (The Holy Bible, English Standard Version®), copyright © 2001
by Crossway, a publishing ministry of Good News Publishers. Used by permission. All rights reserved.

ISBN 978-1-4347-0992-9
eISBN 978-1-4347-1225-7

© 2017 James Warner Wallace
Published in association with the literary agency of Mark Sweeney & Associates, Bonita Springs, FL 34135.

Illustrations by J. Warner Wallace
The Team: Tim Peterson, Amy Konyndyk, Nick Lee, Jack Campbell, Susan Murdock
Cover Design: Jon Middel
Cover Photo: Getty Images

Printed in the United States of America

First Edition 2017

2 3 4 5 6 7 8 9 10 11

061417

CONTENTS

Go to **www.ForensicFaithBook.com** to download a free
facilitator's guide to help coordinate a group study with
the *Forensic Faith* curriculum kit. Now available.

Session One
WHY DO YOU BELIEVE?

I understand what it's like to be in the right place *accidentally*. As I travel to speaking engagements in cold and remote areas, I'm increasingly grateful to have been born and raised in sunny Southern California, where it is 75 degrees and dry nearly every day. California has great beaches and many recreational, educational, and employment opportunities. But if you quiz me about the nature of California, you'll quickly discover I am not a well-informed resident.

I don't know what year California was founded or how many counties it has. I don't know how many people live here, the exact procedure for how a bill is passed, or how the state legislature is organized. What's the state bird, tree, flower, or motto? I can't tell you. When it comes right down to it, I'm a pretty terrible Californian given how little I know about my own state. But make no mistake about it. I'm a Californian. I was born and raised here.

When it comes to our spiritual "residency," I find many people are Christians the same way I'm a Californian. They were born and raised in the church yet are unable to answer any of the pressing questions people might ask about Christianity. Maybe these believers had an experience that convinced them Christianity was true. Maybe they are "in the right place" but are not quite sure *why* it's the right place. Their affiliation with Christianity appears to be more like a *lucky accident* than an *informed decision*.

For me, that was problematic. For most of my life I was not a believer. In fact, I was a very committed atheist. I was skeptical of people who believed something simply because they grew up a certain way or had an "experience." I wasn't raised in a Christian home, and the man I respected most (my father) was a cynical detective. He was (and still is) a steadfast atheist. I wasn't about to trust something I couldn't examine evidentially.

It troubled me that members of *every* religious group seemed to give the same answers many of my Christian friends did for why they held their beliefs. From Buddhist to Mormon to Baptist, people typically offered the same responses. Yet it isn't possible for these conflicting claims about God and reality to be true; they could all be *wrong*, or *one* could be correct, but they cannot *all* be correct. So I set out to investigate and test the claims of Christianity based on the evidence. Long story short, I found them to be true.

Today we live in a culture that is increasingly skeptical of Christianity—perhaps even more than I was. If we want others to believe Christianity is true, then our answers cannot sound like the answers given by every other religious group. We must have answers that stand up to aggressive challenges. We must embrace the *evidence* for what we believe, building what I call a *forensic faith*.

OPEN THE CASE FILE
(5 MINUTES – CONSIDER AND ANSWER THE QUESTIONS)

When we, as Christians, share what we believe with the people we encounter, we're likely to be asked a version of the question "Why are you a Christian?"

1. In what way have *you* answered that question when it has been asked of you?

_____

_____

_____

2. To what degree did your answer satisfy the person who asked you?

_____

_____

_____

How satisfied are *you* with your answer?

_____

 **VIEW THE VIDEO TESTIMONY**
(11 MINUTES – TAKE NOTES)

"Testing" the truths of Christianity

_____

_____

Why people say they are Christians

_____

_____

Experience versus *evidence*—how we can know what is true

_____

_____

 **CONDUCT A GROUP INVESTIGATION**
(23 MINUTES – INVESTIGATE THE ISSUES AND ANSWER THE QUESTIONS)

When I ask people the question, "Why are you a Christian?" I seldom, if ever, hear someone respond, "I am a Christian because it is *true*." Few people seem to have taken the time to investigate the evidence to determine if the claims of Christianity are true. Although intuition and experience may incline us to believe, they don't allow us to differentiate whether Christianity or any other religion is actually true. A faith that is based on experience alone, rather than grounded in objective evidence, often fails to persuade others or withstand aggressive opposition.

1 To what extent do you share the concerns raised in the video about the nature and reliability of our Christian testimony—*why* we believe *what* we believe?

_____

_____

_____

2 Why do you think it is important for each of us to be certain that the claims of Christianity are *true?*

_____

_____

_____

3 On a scale of one (low) to ten (high), how capable do you think most Christians are of intellectually defending their Christian beliefs, and why do you believe this to be the case?

_____

_____

_____

Why is it important for Christ followers today to be articulate about the truth of Christian beliefs and practices?

_____

_____

_____

 4 What impact does our ability to defend Christian beliefs have on:

Our willingness and ability to engage in dynamic dialogue with people who are not believers and answer their pressing questions about Christianity?

_____

_____

_____

Our testimony and reputation in our culture?

_____

_____

_____

WHY DO PEOPLE BELIEVE?

Typically, people respond to the question "Why are you a Christian?" in one of the following broad categories:

Answer 1:
I was raised in the church.
My parents were Christians.
I've been a Christian as long as I can remember.

Answer 2:
I've had an experience that convinced me.
The Holy Spirit confirmed it for me.
God demonstrated His existence to me.

Answer 3:
I was changed by Jesus.
I used to be [fill in your choice of immoral lifestyle], and God changed my life.

Answer 4:
Because I just know the Bible is true.
Because God called me to believe.

These are the same kinds of answers people of many faiths give. If you're a Christian simply because you've been raised in the church, how can you be sure Christianity is true? If you're a Christian because you've had a transformative experience, how do you know if this experience is truly from the God of the Bible?

In what way(s) have you seen people who do not believe in Christ respond when we explain our beliefs primarily in terms of our personal experiences? When we explain Christianity in terms of evidential truth?

_____

_____

_____

How much does it concern you that the majority of young people who have been raised in the church abandon their faith during their college years, and what might be done to address this trend?

_____

_____

_____

The apostle Peter said that if we are Christians, we are called to serve one another with "sympathy, brotherly love, a tender heart, and a humble mind" (1 Peter 3:8 ESV). Furthermore, he said that we are called to protect the truth by "being prepared to make a defense to anyone who asks you for a reason for the hope that is in you" (1 Peter 3:15 ESV). What have you learned today about what is required of us if we are to serve and protect the message of Christ in our culture?

_____

_____

_____

 What changes in our beliefs and faith practices do you think are necessary to fulfill this calling?

_____

_____

_____

 ## TAKE A PERSONAL ASSESSMENT
(5 MINUTES – EXAMINE YOUR OWN SITUATION AND ANSWER THE QUESTIONS)

As you consider your Christian faith, to what extent are your beliefs based on your experiences? Your upbringing? Evidence you've discovered? God's calling?

_____

_____

_____

 Would you then describe your faith as primarily *accidental* or *evidential*? Why?

_____

_____

_____

When it comes to explaining *why* you believe *what* you believe, what do you think is lacking, out of balance, or indefensible?

_____

_____

_____

What impact have the reasons supporting your beliefs had on your ability to share (or not share) the claims of Christianity with other people?

_____

_____

_____

Would you describe yourself as a Christ follower who is (1) basically anti-intellectual, (2) open to learning evidence supporting Christianity yet unprepared to share such evidence, or (3) actively pursuing the ability to make the case for your Christian beliefs confidently, knowing that the claims of Christianity are built on the Bible and can be supported by true evidence?

_____

_____

In what ways has your approach to your Christian faith influenced people around you in positive or negative ways? (Be honest.)

_____

_____

_____

What steps are you willing to take in order to more fully worship God with all your heart, soul, and mind?

_____

_____

_____

FORM A STRATEGIC PLAN
(5 MINUTES - EXAMINE YOUR CALENDAR AND CREATE AN ACTION PLAN)

How willing are you to learn more about why you believe what you believe—to embrace a more rigorously intellectual faith—not only for your own benefit but also to help you come alongside those Christians whose faith is under attack, those who have rejected Christianity's claims, or those who have walked away from Christianity because they were unaware of the evidence?

_____

_____

_____

Which person(s) in your sphere of influence—a friend, family member, coworker, neighbor—has walked away from Christianity because it seemed to lack the evidence to support its claims?

_____

_____

_____

What is your greatest concern for that person?

_____

_____

_____

What do you think your role may be in reaching out to that person and sharing why the claims of Christianity are worth believing?

_____

_____

_____

Good intentions rarely take us very far in our efforts. Are you willing to make a strategic plan of action and commit your plan to a date on a calendar? If so, write down a date this week, _____, when you will initiate a plan of action to begin addressing the evidential concerns of the person(s) you identified above.

MAKE A CLOSING STATEMENT
(1 MINUTE – CONTEMPLATE AND PRAY)

Now, more than ever, Christians must shift from *accidental belief* to *evidential trust*. It's time to know *why* we believe *what* we believe. Despite the decline of Christianity in our culture, it's not too late to learn how to approach our Christian beliefs evidentially and take the same forensic approach a detective takes when examining an event from the past. We can be confident that the evidence will support the claims of Christianity.

Dear God, we thank You for Your gift of salvation and the hope we have of eternal life with You. We know You want us to share this good news with all people. Please teach us as we take this opportunity to learn how to "make the case" for Christianity. Help us realize why Christian case making is so important—for us in our spiritual growth and confidence, and for those who need to be shown evidence for the claims of Christ so that they may come into a personal relationship with You. In Jesus's name we pray, amen.

CONDUCT A SECONDARY INVESTIGATION
(60 MINUTES – READ FOR BETTER UNDERSTANDING)

To better understand the issues raised in this session, read the preface to *Forensic Faith: A Homicide Detective Makes the Case for a More Reasonable, Evidential Christian Faith*, "To

Protect and to Serve" (pages 19 to 29). Take notes specifically for the following section of the preface:

The Case for Case Making (page 25)

_____

_____

_____

_____

_____

_____

_____

_____

Session Two
DISTINCTIVE DUTY

During the first five years of my law enforcement career, I was challenged at every turn, in part because my father—also named Jim Wallace—was a police officer in the same department. In addition to being "Wallace's college kid," I was an honor recruit. My peers wanted to test how much I really knew about life on the streets, and they set the bar high. At times I feared I would fall short of everyone's expectations.

Could I handle tough situations? Was I too soft? How well did I know the law? Would I recognize a crime when I saw it? Could I put together a case?

Under the intense scrutiny, I soon discovered that the demands of a successful law enforcement career required me to be "all in" or "all out." When I accepted my public duty as a police officer and my personal calling as a member of the Wallace family, I had a choice: accept the challenges and rise to meet them, or simply shrink back into irrelevance and obscurity. There was no middle ground. I had to decide whether law enforcement was *critically* important or *unimportant* to me.

Anyone who is a member of the Christian family faces a similar set of challenges. We are sons or daughters of the King, and we've been awarded the gift of eternal life. Our culture is increasingly suspicious of our family affiliation and our status as believers, so it is eager to test us. It demands evidence for what we claim. The bar is set high.

Will we be too soft? Can we handle tough situations? How thoroughly do we know what we believe? Can we present a strong, evidential case for Christianity? To succeed in the hostile environment of our culture, we need to accept the challenges and rise to meet them, or shrink back into irrelevance and obscurity.

Police officers understand their duty to serve and protect, and they are committed to prepare for and fulfill that mission. As Christians, we can learn from law enforcement's resolute approach to *mission*. We, also, have a duty to fulfill. We must understand and accept our role as servants and protectors of the Christian faith. If we believe Christianity is true, it's our obligation to serve others by sharing evidential truth with them. Eternity hangs in the balance.

Each of us needs to be ready to accept our public duty as ambassadors of Jesus Christ in the same way we accept our personal calling as members of God's family. Every day is a call to action, so we must decide whether our Christian affiliation is *unimportant* or *critically* important. We'll never succeed if we are halfhearted in our efforts to make the case for what we believe.

OPEN THE CASE FILE
(4 MINUTES – CONSIDER AND ANSWER THE QUESTIONS)

Most Christians have a "list" of duties that we consider to be an essential part of our faith identity. It is, for example, our duty to obey God's commands, love our neighbor, and share the good news of the gospel with others.

 Have you ever viewed your ability to build a solid, evidence-based case for why you believe what you believe as an essential part of your Christian identity and duty? Why or why not?

_____

_____

 If you were required to testify for the truth of Christianity, what could you offer beyond your own subjective personal experience? What kind of objective evidence could you readily present?

_____

_____

VIEW THE VIDEO TESTIMONY
(13 MINUTES - TAKE NOTES)

Our duty to make the case for Christianity

_____

_____

_____

Jesus: "If you don't believe Me, believe the evidence"

_____

_____

_____

Three types of faith

Unreasonable:

_____

_____

Blind:

_____

_____

Forensic:

_____

_____

Evidence doesn't answer everything; we still need faith

_____

_____

 **CONDUCT A GROUP INVESTIGATION**
(23 MINUTES – INVESTIGATE THE ISSUES AND ANSWER THE QUESTIONS)

Reason and evidence are part of our Christian tradition. Christian history is filled with examples of people who embraced a forensic faith and made the case for Christianity. They modeled for us what it means to be Christian case makers. There is much we can learn from these role models as we embrace evidential case making as part of our Christian identity and duty.

Shouldn't we, as Christians today, know why our beliefs are true and be willing to defend what we believe? Unlike other faiths, Christianity is not based merely on a spiritual idea or concept; it is based on a verifiable, historical event—the death and resurrection of Jesus. It's time for the distinctly evidential nature of Christianity to result in a distinctly intelligent, reasonable, and evidential family of believers. So, let's take a look at our evidential history.

To what extent were you surprised to hear Jesus described as a case maker, a consummate evidentialist?

_____

_____

_____

Which examples can you think of when Jesus used evidence in His teaching to back up His claims? (If you need some help, see John 5:31–32, 36–38; 10:22–27, 31–33, 37–39; 14:11.)

_____

_____

_____

What in these passages indicates that Jesus successfully made His case (even if not all of His listeners believed)?

_____

_____

_____

According to John 20:30–31 and Acts 1:1–3, Jesus (who knew His followers needed more than His direct testimony) stayed with His disciples for forty days after His resurrection. What did He continue to do during that time and for what reason?

_____

_____

When John the Baptist was in prison and experienced nagging doubts concerning Jesus's identity and claims to deity, what did Jesus offer as an antidote to doubt? (See Luke 7:20–23.)

_____

_____

How did the visible evidence—the miracles of healing—build the case for Jesus's identity as the Messiah? (See Isaiah 29:18 and 35:5–6.)

_____

_____

After Thomas, one of Jesus's twelve handpicked disciples, doubted the testimony of others that Jesus had risen from the dead, what evidence did Jesus provide, and what impact did it have on Thomas? (See John 20:24–28.)

_____

_____

What admonition did Jesus give to Thomas concerning the privilege and duty of being an eyewitness of Jesus's ministry? (See John 20:29–31.)

_____

_____

_____

Why were eyewitnesses of Jesus's ministry so important to the development of the early Christian faith—and to people today who receive their eyewitness testimony through the pages of Scripture?

_____

_____

_____

In what ways do you think Jesus's commitment to case making aided His commissioned disciples who relied on their evidential status as eyewitnesses in carrying His message into a hostile world? (See Luke 24:44–48; John 1:6–7.)

_____

_____

_____

| Christ the Case Maker | The Commissioned Case Makers | The Canonical Case Makers | The Continuing Case Makers | The Contemporary Case Makers |

The Rich, Evidential History of Christian Case-Making

What did Jesus ask in His prayer (recorded in John 17:20–21) concerning people like us who believe in Him not because of evidence we have seen with our own eyes but because of the eyewitness testimony (direct evidence) offered by the disciples?

_____

_____

_____

_____

_____

_____

Given all the ways the apostles could have shared the gospel message, they made the case based on their own eyewitness testimony, and many people came to faith based on this evidential approach. In what ways did the evidence of their testimony play a role in your acceptance of the Christian faith?

_____

_____

_____

_____

FOR FURTHER CONSIDERATION

Evidence mattered to the earliest believers.

They trusted the accounts offered by John and Matthew because these men knew Jesus personally. These disciples provided direct evidence (eyewitness testimony) in their gospels.

The early church embraced Luke's gospel based on his evidential, investigative approach. Luke interviewed the eyewitnesses and included their testimony.

Even Mark's gospel was accepted based on its eyewitness value. Although Mark may not have known Jesus personally, his gospel, according to the first-century bishop Papias of Hierapolis, was the accurate collection of testimony from an important eyewitness, Simon Peter.

The apostles (and the men who wrote about them) understood their evidential, case-making role in the earliest Christian communities.

TAKE A PERSONAL ASSESSMENT

(4 MINUTES – EXAMINE YOUR OWN SITUATION AND ANSWER THE QUESTIONS)

Take a few minutes to review the following definitions of *faith*:

Unreasonable Faith: Believing in something *in spite of* the evidence.

We hold an unreasonable belief when we refuse to accept or acknowledge evidence that clearly refutes what we believe is true. The claim "touching a toad will cause warts" is an excellent example. Evidence shows that viruses, not toads, cause warts. So, people who still believe they can contract warts from toads hold an unreasonable belief.

In a similar way, unreasonable *faith* results in believing something is true when evidence can disprove it. Jesus did not ask His followers to ignore the world around them or ignore evidence that might refute His claims. In fact, to this day, there isn't any evidence disproving the eyewitness accounts recorded in the Gospels.

Blind Faith: Believing in something *without* any evidence.

We hold a blind belief when we accept a claim even though we are unaware of any evidence supporting it. I believe, for example, that James David Wallace Sr. is my biological father, even though I am unaware of any existing data that would prove this. I may be right about our biological relationship, or I may be wrong; I would only know *for sure* if I were to see DNA test results.

Similarly, blind *faith* sometimes results in believing something that's true, but it can also result in believing something that's false if there's evidence to prove that the claim is untrue. Jesus did not ask His followers to believe without evidence. In fact, He repeatedly provided evidence to support His claims.

Forensic Faith: Believing in something *because* of the evidence.

We hold a forensic belief when we believe something because it is the most reasonable inference from evidence, although we may still have unanswered questions about the claim. I believe, for example, that amoxicillin can fight bacterial infections. Laboratory evidence supports this claim, and I've used the drug to fight infections. I still don't know how (or why) it works, but I have faith in amoxicillin, even though I have unanswered questions about it.

Similarly, Jesus encouraged us to have a forensic faith based on the evidence He provided. He knew we would still have unanswered questions, but He wanted us to be able to defend what we believe (and guard the truth of Christianity) in hostile public settings.

What examples have you seen of unreasonable faith, blind faith, and forensic faith, and how have these different types of faith influenced (for better or worse) your Christian commitment and growth?

_____

_____

_____

_____

_____

_____

_____

_____

_____

1 Of these definitions of *faith*, which is the best description of your faith today?

_____

_____

_____

_____

2 How satisfied are you with your answer?

_____

_____

_____

_____

3 What changes do you want to make in how you embrace your faith—for your benefit? For the benefit of those who do not yet know Jesus?

_____

_____

_____

_____

FORM A STRATEGIC PLAN
(5 MINUTES – EXAMINE YOUR CALENDAR AND CREATE AN ACTION PLAN)

Now that you have completed the group study, consider again the question asked at the beginning of this study session: If you were required to testify and make a case for the truth of Christianity, what could you offer beyond your own subjective experiences? What kind of objective evidence could you present, for example, to make the case for the Bible's reliability or God's existence?

_____

_____

_____

_____

These questions bring us to the bigger question each of us must answer for ourselves: "Am I prepared to give an answer—to make a case—to everyone who asks me to give a reason for the hope I have?" If someone asked me to make a case for the reliability of the New Testament, what kind of evidence would I consider? Can I articulate the archaeological evidence? Can I describe the internal textual evidence from the Gospels? Am I familiar with early, non-Christian sources related to the life and ministry of Jesus?

_____

_____

_____

_____

Don't feel bad if you don't think you're adequately prepared; that's why we're doing this study in the first place. And that's why these next few questions are so important:

How willing are you to examine carefully the evidence for your Christian beliefs? In what ways are you undertaking the distinctive Christian duty of thoughtfully seeking evidence for Christianity so you know why your beliefs are true, and can willingly defend what you believe?

_____

_____

_____

_____

_____

I hope and pray that you will take to heart 2 Timothy 3:14: "You, however, continue in the things you have learned and become convinced of, knowing from whom you have learned them." Subject your beliefs to rational exploration and reasonable examination so you will be fully convinced they are true. The biblical authors had nothing to hide. They confidently challenged their listeners to investigate their claims.

The Bible was written on the authority of eyewitness accounts, and there are many additional resources to help you examine the biblical evidence and the reliability of the New Testament:

Cold-Case Christianity: A Homicide Detective Investigates the Claims of the Gospels
by J. Warner Wallace (David C Cook, 2013)
The Case for Christ: A Journalist's Personal Investigation of the Evidence for Jesus
by Lee Strobel (Zondervan, 1998)
The Case for the Resurrection of Jesus
by Gary Habermas and Michael Licona (Kregel, 2004)
The New Testament Documents: Are They Reliable?
by F. F. Bruce (Wm. B. Eerdmans, 2013)
The Testimony of the Evangelists: The Gospels Examined by the Rules of Evidence
by Simon Greenleaf (Kregel Classics, 1995)
Jesus and the Eyewitnesses: The Gospels as Eyewitness Testimony
by Richard Bauckham (Eerdmans, 2006)

Choose a source to study: _____.

Set a date to begin studying the evidence _____.

MAKE A CLOSING STATEMENT
(1 MINUTE – CONTEMPLATE AND PRAY)

Just as police officers are sworn to protect and serve the public, we need to eagerly accept our duty to investigate and discover the truth of Christianity so we can communicate the case to others. Every day is a call to action.

Dear Lord, just as the early disciples of Jesus expressed great zeal for Your truth and boldly made their case based on what they had seen, give us the passion to investigate the evidence for Christianity so we can become effective case makers. May we be faithful to learn and apply the disciplines of forensic faith and to encourage other followers of Jesus to join us. Guide our steps as we recognize and accept our duty as Christians to examine and test what we believe so we are prepared to confidently and boldly share the gospel in our increasingly skeptical and hostile culture. Help us to know what we believe and why we believe it. Help us to model Christian case making for future generations of believers. We ask this in the name of Jesus, amen.

CONDUCT A SECONDARY INVESTIGATION
(60 MINUTES – READ FOR BETTER UNDERSTANDING)

To better understand the issues raised in this session, read chapter 1 in *Forensic Faith: A Homicide Detective Makes the Case for a More Reasonable, Evidential Christian Faith,* "Distinctive Duty: 5 Evidential Examples to Help You Embrace Your Calling as a

Christian Case Maker" (pages 31 to 65). Take notes specifically for the following section of chapter 1:

The Christian *Difference* Is the Foundation of Our Christian *Duty* (page 35)

_____

_____

_____

_____

_____

_____

_____

_____

_____

Session Three
TARGETED TRAINING

"Man down! Man down! Holster your weapons!"

I had been hit several times. My right arm and chest were stinging, and my uniform shirt was covered in red. Fortunately, it was nothing more than paint from our paintball training weapons; I was more embarrassed than injured. As a new member of SWAT, I was the least tenured officer on the team. Although I considered myself to be a good shot, my opponent was a much better, more seasoned marksman. At the end of this latest training scenario, his uniform was unblemished while mine was (yet again) tarnished with red.

The marksman who played the barricaded suspect consistently won those early battles. I seldom hit him in return. We trained for weeks, testing and practicing our tactics. As our training progressed, I made fewer mistakes and my tactics improved. The more we trained, the less I had to wash my uniform. I ultimately mastered my position on the team.

Training in law enforcement tactics is essential because officers *deploy regularly*. If we handled every call for service over the phone and never left the station, we wouldn't need to exercise or train tactically. Training is necessary only because we intend to *deploy*.

The same is true for us as Christians. Sadly, most of us view our church buildings as places to gather on Sunday. Seldom do we think of them as places to prepare and train for our *deployment*—going out to share the good news in the world around us. If our experience as "the church" is limited to meeting in church buildings, there's little reason to engage in meaningful training.

However, we live in a time when the secular culture is more aggressive and the Christian culture is more vulnerable than ever before. We are losing the next generation. By the time they complete college, most of our Christian young people will no longer consider themselves Christians.

We can no longer do "church" as we always have, relying on traditional Sunday school classes and youth programs to pass on the truths of Christianity. Our typical methods of teaching are no longer enough. The numbers don't lie. Few Christians truly understand what Christianity teaches, and even fewer young Christians can articulate what they believe.[1] It is time for us to rethink our *role* so that we can rethink our *response*. It is time to stop *teaching* and start *training*.

 OPEN THE CASE FILE
(4 MINUTES – CONSIDER AND ANSWER THE QUESTIONS)

Think about what it takes to learn something new or to prepare ourselves to do something significant (especially if we've never done it before). What might be the best ways for a person to prepare to achieve an important and challenging goal?

_____

_____

_____

What are the limitations of teaching ourselves to successfully accomplish something new just by reading a book, watching a video, or taking a class or two?

_____

_____

_____

Which additional steps might we need to take, or what kind of a process might we need to engage, to adequately prepare and achieve our goal?

_____

_____

_____

VIEW THE VIDEO TESTIMONY
(13 MINUTES – TAKE NOTES)

Teaching isn't enough

_____

_____

Training makes the difference

_____

_____

      "T" _____

      _____

      _____

      "R" _____

      _____

      _____

      "A" _____

      _____

      _____

      "I" _____

      _____

      _____

      "N" _____

      _____

      _____

CONDUCT A GROUP INVESTIGATION

(23 MINUTES – INVESTIGATE THE ISSUES AND ANSWER THE QUESTIONS)

I hadn't been a Christian for very long when I was asked to teach my son's third-grade Sunday school class. Fortunately, we had an excellent curriculum, and I learned quickly. I eventually entered seminary, and by the time I graduated, I was a high school youth pastor. The ministry grew quickly and seemed successful, but just months after my first group of seniors graduated, I got a shocking wake-up call. All but one of those seniors had walked away from their faith by winter break of their first year in college. I felt like a complete failure. Something had to change, and I knew what it was: we needed to stop teaching. You see, in the church we have lots of teachers and concerned parents who want to teach their kids, but the teaching we have done for generations has become ineffective. While we've been *teaching*, students have been leaving the faith. We need to stop *teaching* and start *training*.

The apostle Paul, in one of his instructive letters to Timothy, wrote, "All Scripture is inspired by God and profitable for teaching …" but Paul didn't stop there. He continued, "… for reproof, for correction, for training in righteousness; so that the man of God may be adequate, equipped for every good work" (2 Timothy 3:16–17). Paul considered it important to make a clear distinction between teaching and training. How would you describe the differences between teaching and training?

_____

_____

_____

_____

_____

_____

_____

1 What does training provide that teaching does not?

_____

_____

_____

_____

2 Why, then, is training important if we are to successfully protect and proclaim the truth claims of Christianity?

_____

_____

_____

_____

The T-R-A-I-N paradigm:

"T" – Test Yourself and Those You Love

As I experienced in law enforcement, a bar fight with a training officer in tow for backup is a great setting for testing the ability of less experienced police officers. What kind of controlled settings might be good for testing our ability as Christians to defend our beliefs and motivating us to become better equipped for case making?

_____

_____

_____

What can we learn about ourselves when we test our case-making abilities, and how essential is this knowledge?

_____

_____

_____

"R" – Raise the Bar and Surprise Yourself

Many of us make a significant investment in our professional (and, yes, our recreational) proficiency. We earn degrees and certificates, we train for fitness, we compete to be the very best. But how high do we set the bar for ourselves when it comes to protecting and serving the Christian message?

_____

_____

How much do we need to "up our game" in terms of the challenges we are willing to take on?

_____

_____

_____

How much will we require of ourselves so that we can become proficient case makers?

_____

_____

_____

"A" – Arm Yourself for Battle

A police officer has access to the tools—pistol, handcuffs, baton, and more—necessary to do the job. And a police officer is trained to use these tools effectively. If God's truth is the most effective tool we have to defend the Christian faith, what must we know about the evidence for God's existence, the reliability of the Bible, and the truth claims of the Christian worldview in order to defend it?

_____

_____

_____

What level of commitment is required for us to be trained in the truths of the Christian faith and to learn how to use that knowledge in the heat of battle?

_____

_____

_____

What are the risks if we know the truth but isolate ourselves from the battle-field of secular culture?

_____

_____

_____

What are some ways we can begin to address opposing claims a little at a time so that we are inoculated—prepared and protected—when we make the case for Christianity and face an onslaught of opposition?

_____

_____

_____

 "I" – Involve Yourself and Hit the Streets

No training is complete without hands-on experience. To make the most of such training, we must engage the power of the *calendar*. Events on a calendar provide incentive to make things happen. Think about it. How differently do we prepare for something that has a specific deadline as opposed to something we will do when we get around to it?

_____

_____

If you want to transform your effectiveness as a Christian case maker, commit your training to a calendar. What kind of commitments and opportunities do you think should be included on a training calendar?

_____

_____

_____

_____

_____

"N" – Nurture Others by Demonstrating the Nature of Jesus

There is more to Christian case making than having the knowledge and becoming adept at using it. First Peter 3:15–16 instructs us not only to share the reason for our hope but to do so with "gentleness and respect" (ESV). Why do you think it is important for Christian case makers to reflect the character of Jesus through gentleness and respect even while we are fully engaged on the battlefield?

NO SUBSTITUTE FOR TRAINING

When you repeatedly perform the same physical process over and over again, your actions become a matter of muscular "habit." Your body almost seems to work on its own, responding from "muscle memory" rather than reacting to mental commands. Muscle memory is important to police officers because we face unpredictable situations that often involve complications such as weapon failures. We're far more likely to succeed if we can resolve failures and unexpected situations by muscle memory. So we train. We repeatedly conduct failure drills. And when the pressure is on, we resort to our training.

For the same reason, the best Christian case makers are those who continually engage the culture and respond to the challenges levied by unbelievers. Every interaction is a training opportunity. The more you engage, the more you train, and the more your case-making efforts become a part of your muscle memory.

_____

_____

What often happens to the case for Christianity when Christians respond in harsh, unloving ways to those who oppose them?

_____

_____

_____

_____

Why is it important for leaders or trainers of Christian case makers to be prepared to be gentle and respectful of those who are wounded or have become discouraged during their training to become Christian case makers?

_____

_____

_____

_____

_____

TAKE A PERSONAL ASSESSMENT
(4 MINUTES – EXAMINE YOUR OWN SITUATION AND ANSWER THE QUESTIONS)

I often get email from readers of my website. One young man, Andrew Deane, wrote to me about some of his experiences in college that show how high the stakes are for Christian case making. He described professors who explained away the "mythology" of Jesus, attacked the concept of intelligent design, argued for the existence of aliens but refused to acknowledge the existence of God, and so on. He wrote:

> Unfortunately, most of our fellow brothers and sisters in Christ are severely lacking in training, and when they encounter even the weakest arguments, they are not prepared … As a Christian in the college setting, you are being constantly challenged, constantly poked and prodded. It is easy to throw your hands in the air, becoming convinced your faith is a lie … All Christians, but especially ones in college, must know what they believe and why they believe it if they have any hope of surviving with their faith intact … I think of college almost like an atheist ambush. The Christians are walking in totally unaware of the danger until it is too late and the damage has already been done.

That's why I wanted to take the time to thank you … When I entered college, I was struggling with many of the objections I encountered. I discovered your podcast and your careful research. The evidentiary approach was incredibly helpful. As a result, I actually exited college with my faith even stronger than when I began.[2]

If what we believe about Christianity is true, we have an obligation to make the case to the best of our ability. Eternity hangs in the balance. We must train so that we can become effective case makers. Training is more than mere instruction. Training involves putting instruction into practice in order to become proficient.

To what degree have you been putting what you've learned as a Christian into practice?

_____

_____

_____

How proficient would you say you are at understanding and explaining to others why you believe what you believe, and what are you willing to do to become better trained?

_____

_____

_____

Which obstacles to training stand in your path, and how might you overcome them?

_____

_____

_____

_____

Consider how you use your discretionary time. Which of your daily life priorities and activities need to be rearranged so that training can be a real part of your Christian faith?

_____

_____

How much time are you willing to set aside each week to read and study the evidence for Christianity?

_____

_____

_____

What time each month will you dedicate to practical application of what you have learned?

_____

_____

_____

FORM A STRATEGIC PLAN
(5 MINUTES – EXAMINE YOUR CALENDAR AND CREATE AN ACTION PLAN)

Are you ready to give an account for the hope that is in you? Then start by taking the test. The test, The Forensic Faith Readiness Review, is a simple, seven-question survey. It's located at the back of this workbook. The Forensic Faith Readiness Review will help you evaluate your strengths and weaknesses as a Christian case maker.

Set a date to take the test now: _____.

After you answer the questions in the Forensic Faith Readiness Review, make an honest assessment of your answers. Did you struggle to articulate an answer? Were some of your answers more persuasive than others? Don't be discouraged. The purpose of the review is to provide a starting point from which you can begin to improve and grow in your case-making skills. The next step is to identify where you need to start training and set a date.

I will start training by studying the following (or taking this action):

_____

_____

I will devote _____ hours each week to this endeavor, beginning on this date: _____.

MAKE A CLOSING STATEMENT
(1 MINUTE – CONTEMPLATE AND PRAY)

If you're a Christian, you're part of an important team. You have a duty, a family obligation, and a mission. You're called to embrace a forensic faith so that you can make the case for what you believe and contend for the faith. Now it's time to participate in targeted training so that you can learn how to investigate the case for Christianity and communicate it to others.

Dear Lord, You have called us to guard and proclaim Your truth so that all people will receive the gift of salvation You offer. Forgive us for our lack of commitment and diligence in fulfilling our role as Christian case makers. May we be willing to stretch our knowledge, train rigorously, and test our character so that we are prepared to contend for the faith in a hostile culture. Help us to faithfully represent You well as we make a defense to everyone who asks us to give an account for the hope that is within us. In Jesus's name we pray, amen.

CONDUCT A SECONDARY INVESTIGATION
(60 MINUTES – READ FOR BETTER UNDERSTANDING)

To better understand the issues raised in this session, read chapter 2 in *Forensic Faith: A Homicide Detective Makes the Case for a More Reasonable, Evidential Christian Faith*, "Targeted Training: 5 Steps toward Preparing Yourself to Protect and Serve as a First Responder" (pages 67 to 94). Take notes specifically for the following section of chapter 2:

"Muscle Memory" and Christian Case Making (page 93)

_____

_____

_____

_____

_____

_____

_____

_____

INTENSE INVESTIGATION, PART 1

Thinking about Evidence and
Learning to Take Notes

In 1981 Mike Lubahn told police that Carol, his twenty-seven-year-old wife and mother of their two young children, had run away from home. Everyone believed Mike's story, including Carol's family and the original detective who considered this to be nothing more than a missing person's case. More than thirty years later, however, after a long cold-case investigation, we convicted Mike of Carol's murder.

A week after the verdict, Keith Morrison, anchor of NBC's *Dateline*, challenged my conclusions. While we were taping another *Dateline* episode, Keith leaned back in his chair and said, "I'm not so sure you've got the right guy this time." His right elbow was propped against his crossed left arm, and he was cradling his chin in his right hand. I'd seen this mischievous, questioning expression often as we chronicled many of my cold cases. "Come on, Jim. What makes you so sure Mike's the killer?"

His doubt was understandable. It had been an incredibly difficult case. Our agency didn't begin working the case as a homicide until six years after the murder. We never found a single piece of physical evidence. There were still many unanswered questions. We didn't know how he did it, where he did it, how he disposed of the body, or how he moved the car. In spite of the unanswered questions, the jury found Mike guilty after approximately four hours of deliberation.

"This case is just like all the other cases, Keith," I explained. "It's not any *one* thing that demonstrates Mike's guilt. It's the collection of *everything* that demonstrates his guilt."

Even though some questions remained unanswered, I had more than enough evidence to confidently conclude that Mike was guilty.

As it turned out, weeks after the taping and prior to the final edit of the episode, Mike Lubahn removed any doubt about his guilt. At his sentencing hearing he confessed to the crime and revealed where he had buried Carol.

How could I be so confident when we didn't have all the answers? It's really quite simple: evidential confidence is often the result of investigative diligence. I was confident of Mike's guilt because I did what I always do: I took the necessary, time-tested investigative steps to evaluate the case, collect evidence, and come to a reasonable conclusion.

I've learned to trust the investigative process—not just in my cold cases, but in investigating the truth claims of Christianity. Our confidence in the truth of Christianity can be bolstered if we apply investigative diligence to our faith.

OPEN THE CASE FILE

(5 MINUTES – CONSIDER AND ANSWER THE QUESTIONS)

It is not uncommon for people who reject the Christian faith to insist that there is no real evidence for Jesus's claim that He was God—or that He even existed. How do you respond when someone makes such a claim? How do you know for certain that their claim is false?

_____

_____

_____

How is it possible to gather enough evidence to make a case for Jesus when thousands of years have passed since He lived on this earth?

_____

_____

_____

VIEW THE VIDEO TESTIMONY
(11 MINUTES – TAKE NOTES)

Cold-case investigation and Christian case making—surprising similarities

_____

_____

_____

_____

Building the case on the basis of evidence

_____

_____

_____

Study the "casebook" from cover to cover

_____

_____

_____

Extraordinary claims and ordinary evidence

_____

_____

_____

Take notes and analyze data

_____

_____

_____

_____

CONDUCT A GROUP INVESTIGATION

(23 MINUTES – INVESTIGATE THE ISSUES AND ANSWER THE QUESTIONS)

Once we've accepted our evidential duty concerning Christianity's claims and embraced a commitment to training, we need to learn to think like cold-case detectives. Cold cases involve events that occurred in the distant past. None of my cases have ever benefited from DNA or other forensic evidence, which is often why they went cold in the first place. Original eyewitnesses may have died. Detectives who chronicled eyewitness statements at the time of the crime may also have died or are unavailable. So, as I reopen each case, I have the difficult task of trying to determine what happened, even though the original witnesses and the report writers are likely to be long dead.

Does that sound familiar? The New Testament Gospels present a similar challenge. As Christians, we want to understand what happened in the distant past, even though we don't have the equivalent of DNA or forensic evidence or have access to the original eyewitnesses or gospel authors. Although this may seem daunting, the skills and practices of a cold-case detective can make it easier.

As you watched the video, what did you notice about the similarities between investigating a cold case and making the case for Christ? What did you notice about the similarities between a casebook and the Bible?

_____

_____

In what ways does understanding the case-making process help you to consider how to practice a forensic faith?

_____

_____

_____

What did you realize about the nature of evidence, particularly the value of cumulative, circumstantial, or indirect evidence when building a case?

_____

_____

 How might this help you defend the Christian faith as true?

_____

_____

_____

Employing Investigative Practices:

 Investigative Practice #1 – Read the Casebook Completely

When beginning a new investigation, it is necessary to read the casebook from cover to cover—every crime report, investigative summary, eyewitness interview transcript, autopsy report, and crime-scene investigation report. The objective is to understand the casebook as if we were part of the *original* investigation. Considering the effort it takes for investigators to repeatedly read, dissect, reorganize, and eventually understand a casebook, how much of a commitment is required for a person to become an expert Christian case maker?

_____

_____

_____

What are your thoughts as you consider making a commitment to Christian case making, and what are the obstacles that might cause you (and likely many other Christians) to step away from the challenge of developing a forensic faith?

_____

_____

_____

Which tools have you found to be most helpful in understanding the historical flow and theological connections in the Bible?

_____

_____

_____

> **READ YOUR "CASEBOOK," THE BIBLE**
>
> If you want to develop a forensic faith, you'll need to take a detective's approach to our Christian "casebook," the Bible. That may appear to be a daunting task, but it can be done in just one year. Many free Bible-reading plans are available online to help you stay the course, but if you want to keep it simple, commit to reading four chapters a day. At that pace, you'll finish the entire Bible in a year, even if you get busy and miss sixty days along the way.

What is at risk when we ignore the context of evidence from the Bible?

_____

_____

_____

Investigative Practice #2 – Think about the Nature of Evidence Broadly

The job of a cold-case detective is to find the evidence prior investigators may have missed. To accomplish the task of building a case for Christianity, we must have an open mind and consider everything for its potential evidential value so that we don't miss anything. When we examine the case for Christianity, what kinds of evidence do we readily recognize as important to building our case?

_____

_____

_____

If we broaden our search to include every potential bit of evidence, what kinds of seemingly less important, ordinary, or more obscure evidence might contribute to making a case for the claims of the Christian faith?

_____

_____

_____

Investigative Practice #3 – Take Notes and Analyze Thoroughly

An investigator finds evidence by studying and taking notes of everything in the casebook and analyzing it. It is helpful to identify different types of evidence, how evidence correlates to specific events, and what witnesses and suspects said or didn't say by their choice of words. When investigating a case, every word matters. When we investigate the Bible, we need to remember that the writers chose their topics and words carefully. So we need to study what is written in detail, taking note of how nouns and pronouns are used, why certain adjectives or adverbs are used, what underlying feelings or motivations are revealed, and whether a particular topic is covered in detail or not at all. Consider, for example, Luke 1:1–4 (ESV):

Inasmuch as many have undertaken to compile a narrative of the things that have been accomplished among us, just as those who from the beginning were eyewitnesses and ministers of the word have delivered them to us, it seemed good to me also, having followed all things closely for some time past, to write an orderly account for you, most excellent Theophilus, that you may have certainty concerning the things you have been taught.

Which words or phrases in this passage might be particularly important for revealing evidence about Luke's subject matter?

_____

_____

_____

Just from this brief passage, what do we learn about Luke's motivation and qualification for writing?

_____

_____

_____

Which words might indicate the quality of work Luke put into his writing?

_____

_____

_____

What indicates that there might be other writings that provide evidence of the same truths for which Luke gives testimony?

_____

_____

_____

TAKE A PERSONAL ASSESSMENT
(5 MINUTES – EXAMINE YOUR OWN SITUATION AND ANSWER THE QUESTIONS)

Investigators develop and employ particular practices that help them accomplish their goals. When used in this sense, *practice* refers to repeated, customary, or habitual activities. A particular action does not become a practice unless it is done repeatedly or habitually.

If we want to develop a forensic faith, we need to rethink the way we engage our Christian worldview. It isn't enough to read a book or do one Bible study. We have to put what we know and learn into *practice*. We need to start thinking like cold-case detectives. We need to embrace the habits that detectives employ to investigate truth.

In which investigative practices am I most skilled, and how might I use them more effectively?

_____

_____

_____

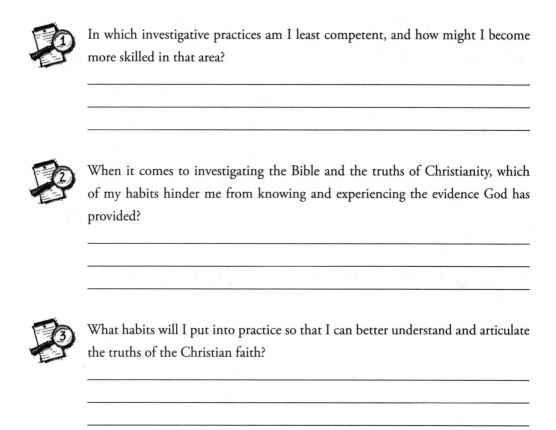

In which investigative practices am I least competent, and how might I become more skilled in that area?

_____

_____

_____

When it comes to investigating the Bible and the truths of Christianity, which of my habits hinder me from knowing and experiencing the evidence God has provided?

_____

_____

_____

What habits will I put into practice so that I can better understand and articulate the truths of the Christian faith?

_____

_____

_____

FORM A STRATEGIC PLAN
(5 MINUTES – EXAMINE YOUR CALENDAR AND CREATE AN ACTION PLAN)

We don't need to find extraordinary evidence in order to build the case for an extraordinary claim. A convincing case that leads to reasonable conclusions can be built with ordinary evidence. Although the claims of Christianity are indeed extraordinary, there is nothing exceptional or unattainable required to investigate or build a case for them. Are you ready to give Christian case making a try—to give it more of your effort?

Start by choosing what could be considered one extraordinary claim of the Christian faith—the existence of God, the resurrection of Jesus, the reliability of the Bible, etc.

I will investigate the extraordinary claim that _____

_____ .

Choose a start date _____ and an end date _____ for your initial investigation.

Then start gathering evidence for that claim. Read your casebook (Bible) thoroughly, keep an open mind for every detail (ordinary as well as extraordinary) that may qualify as evidence, take notes, and analyze the file you are building for everything it can reveal.

MAKE A CLOSING STATEMENT
(1 MINUTE – CONTEMPLATE AND PRAY)

Imagine trying to argue for a conviction on a cold case without the benefit of a casebook. Where would you even start looking for evidence? On what basis would you build a case? How would you have any confidence in your own argument?

_____

_____

_____

But isn't this what many of us who call ourselves Christians try to do when presenting a case for our faith to an unbelieving world? We haven't studied our casebook. Yet somehow we're surprised when our efforts aren't fruitful. We need to get serious about making the case for Christ. We need to get to work and dig deeply into the evidence for Christ that is available in our Bibles.

 Dear Lord, unlike many people in the world, we have easy access to Bibles. We have the opportunity and privilege to investigate what Your Word says whenever we want. Help us not only to recognize how important the Bible is

but to embrace it as Your truth, the foundational evidence we need to build a strong and confident faith. May we take time not only to read it but to study it diligently. Please use what we learn not only to build our faith but to make us competent and confident ambassadors for You in our world. In Jesus's name we pray, amen.

CONDUCT A SECONDARY INVESTIGATION
(60 MINUTES – READ FOR BETTER UNDERSTANDING)

To better understand the issues raised in this session, read the first half of chapter 3 in *Forensic Faith: A Homicide Detective Makes the Case for a More Reasonable, Evidential Christian Faith*, "Intense Investigation: 5 Practices to Help You Examine the Claims of Christianity Like a Good Detective." Read through the first three investigative practices (pages 95 to 117). Take notes specifically for the following section of chapter 3:

The Relationship between *Confidence* and *Diligence* (page 96)

_____

_____

_____

_____

_____

_____

_____

_____

_____

INTENSE INVESTIGATION, PART 2

Organizing the Evidence and Adding to the Case

When investigating a cold case, I organize evidence by making dozens of lists that generally can be categorized as either *evidences* or *explanations*. My lists are purposeful and goal oriented. When an explanation on my list accounts for all the evidence on my other list, the case is solved. This process is called "abductive reasoning." Consider the following example adapted from a case I describe in *Cold-Case Christianity*.

Using some kind of large club, a killer bludgeoned a woman to death in her home. A witness saw a man wearing a mask, blue jeans, and unusual work boots run from the location and drive away in a canary yellow 1972–74 Volkswagen Karmann Ghia. The family suspected her boyfriend, and detectives assembled the following list of evidence:

1. The boyfriend was the same general height and weight as the killer.

2. He lied about his alibi for the night of the murder.

3. Detectives served a search warrant and in the boyfriend's closet discovered a dinged and dented baseball bat that had been soaked in bleach.

4. In his home, they found a pair of dirty blue jeans on which detergent had been used to spot-clean something from the thigh and knee area.

5. There was no sign of forced entry at the woman's home, and the boyfriend was one of three people who had a key.

6. Before the murder, friends had heard him threaten to kill the woman, and after the murder he told detectives he had beaten (but did not admit to killing) his girlfriend on the day of the murder.

7. In the boyfriend's closet, detectives found an unusual pair of boots described by the witness. The boots were manufactured by only one company and sold by only one store in the county. That store had sold only thirty pairs during the past two years.

8. Guilt-ridden, the boyfriend had written an unfinished suicide note that mentioned he was distraught over something horrific he had done on the day of the murder.

9. The boyfriend's car matched the car the witness described.

This list of evidence organizes data in a way that can be assessed and interpreted. It frames a cumulative case argument against the boyfriend. By making lists such as this one, detectives, in essence, *rehearse* the case prior to presenting it to the district attorney for consideration. A written summary of the list helps to answer the question, "Why do you suspect the boyfriend?"

Cumulative case arguments are typically built on multiple pieces of evidence. While these individual pieces might be insufficient to make the case on their own, they become powerful when considered *collectively*. Let's see how we can use the same process to organize the evidence we gather and build a cumulative case for the claims of Christianity.

OPEN THE CASE FILE
(5 MINUTES – CONSIDER AND ANSWER THE QUESTIONS)

When we face any task that overwhelms us—perhaps with information, challenges, important details, possibilities, or a lack of organization—how do we decide where to begin?

_____

_____

① What might be specific steps we would take to make sense of it all and determine a course of action for achieving our goal?

_____

_____

_____

_____

VIEW THE VIDEO TESTIMONY
(12 MINUTES – TAKE NOTES)

Summarize and organize the evidence

_____

_____

Make lists

_____

_____

Assemble the case visually

_____

_____

Gather external, corroborating evidence

_____

_____

The evidence doesn't "say" anything

_____

_____

CONDUCT A GROUP INVESTIGATION
(23 MINUTES – INVESTIGATE THE ISSUES AND ANSWER THE QUESTIONS)

I hope you find it exciting to dig in and start gathering evidence as you examine the truth claims of the Christian faith. I did, and it changed my life. Building a case for Christianity isn't a task we can complete quickly. It takes time. Some of my homicide cold cases have taken more than a decade to solve. And I've been compiling evidence lists in my Bibles for years.

That said, gathering evidence for Christian case making is a process you can learn and benefit from *right away*. Begin by examining topics that intrigue or challenge you; start by investigating the issues your kids, friends, or coworkers have raised when discussing Christianity. Every piece of evidence you collect will strengthen your confidence and make you a better case maker.

Investigative Practice #4 – Summarize and Organize the Evidence

Although many of us may not be familiar with the evidence when we *begin* to investigate a Christian truth claim, we *will be* once we start organizing and listing what we discover. It may seem like a challenge to record our discoveries in a way that is useful. Start by making lists of *evidence* and *explanations*. As you find more evidence, create additional, more specific lists.

For example, if you decided to investigate the claim that Jesus is God, you might make a list of evidence, including places in the Gospels where Jesus was given a divine title or places where Jesus exhibited the power of God. What other kinds of evidence might help you make the case that Jesus is God?

_____

_____

_____

Think for a moment about the foundational Christian truth claims for which you want evidence or want evidence to demonstrate for others. As a group, identify several claims for which you would like to collect evidence. Then, for each claim, identify several lists you might compile as you document and develop your search for evidence and explanations.

Claim:

_____

Kinds of lists you might compile:

_____

_____

_____

Claim:

_____

Kinds of lists you might compile:

_____

_____

_____

Claim:

_____

Kinds of lists you might compile:

_____

_____

_____

Your lists will provide a large quantity of information that needs to be summarized in order to be useful. How might creating a visual diagram of your evidence help you organize it logically so that you can briefly summarize it in a memorable way?

_____

_____

_____

Investigative Practice #5 – Add to the Case Evidentially

Many of my cold cases remained unsolved because there wasn't enough evidence to make the case when the crime was first investigated. Although I begin my investigation by searching for evidence *inside* the casebook, I know I also will need to find corroborating evidence *outside* the casebook.

While the Bible certainly provides sufficient evidence to make the case for Christianity, skeptics who question its reliability often demand evidence from outside sources. What is your initial response to the need to find evidence for the truths *inside* the Bible from sources *outside* the Bible?

_____

_____

_____

_____

Which external sources do you know of that would possibly provide evidence for what is claimed inside the Bible?

_____

_____

_____

There are many external sources of evidence to corroborate what the Bible says. A quick recap includes:

The writings of the early Christian case makers who defended the Christian faith to emperors and other authorities. They cited, among other things, the existence of living people who had been healed by Jesus and the superiority of the Christian worldview in comparison to the worldviews of other cultures. Some of the better known ancient case makers include: Quadratus of Athens (ca. AD 60–129), Aristides of Athens (ca. AD 70–134), Ariston of Pella (ca. AD 100–160), Justin Martyr (ca. AD 100–165), Apollinarius Claudius (ca. AD 100–175), Tertullian (ca. AD 155–240), and Marcus Minucius Felix (ca. AD 180–250).

The writings of ancient pagan and Jewish authors were generally hostile to Christianity. Even these, by addressing the reality of what they sought to deny, actually confirmed many of the claims of Christianity. A partial listing includes: Thallus (ca. AD 5–60), Tacitus (ca. AD 56–117), Mara Bar-Serapion (ca. AD 70–?), Phlegon (ca. AD 80–140), Pliny the Younger (ca. AD 61–113), Suetonius (ca. AD 69–140), Celsus (ca. AD ?–180), Josephus (ca. AD 37–101), and the writers of the Jewish Talmud (AD 400–700).

CORROBORATING EVIDENCE FOR THE BIBLE

Examining the External Evidence

Based on my investigation of the sources listed here, I have written the following summary of evidence for Jesus. This evidence serves to strengthen the case made in the Bible. In fact, if every Bible ever printed were destroyed and the only ancient documents we had mentioning Jesus were those written by hostile non-Christians, we'd still know the following:

Jesus was a real man who lived in history. He was reportedly born of a virgin and had an earthly father who was a carpenter. He lived in Judea, in the region known as Palestine. He was wise and righteous. His teaching was so influential that He developed a large following of Jewish and Gentile disciples. He taught His disciples to live with the same virtue He exhibited, and His moral code was exceedingly high. But Jesus was more than a moral teacher: He possessed "magical powers" and had the ability to predict the future accurately. His supernatural acts and teachings persuaded many Jews to walk away from their Jewish beliefs. Jesus claimed to be God, and His disciples readily accepted this claim. Jewish leaders ultimately brought charges against Jesus based on His actions and teachings. He was prosecuted and crucified under Pontius Pilate during the reign of Tiberius Caesar. There was an earthquake and darkness at the point of the execution. Jesus's followers reported seeing Him resurrected three days after the crucifixion, however, and Jesus even showed them His wounds. His followers believed the resurrection proved Jesus was the Messiah. They adopted Jesus's moral teaching and lived their lives accordingly, holding to their belief in His deity, even though it meant they would suffer greatly at the hands of the Roman Empire. They were ultimately persecuted for their faith in Christ.

How surprised are you that so much external evidence exists? Which of these types of external evidence or writers might you want to investigate further?

_____

_____

How does what you've learned already—just during our discussion time—help you answer skeptics who claim Jesus never existed and that Christianity is merely a fabrication?

_____

_____

_____

What would you say in response to that challenge?

_____

_____

_____

In addition to the strong, historic, evidential record supporting the claims of Christianity, we can also examine evidence for God's existence from other "external" sources. These include cosmological evidence related to the origin and fine-tuning of the universe, biological evidence related to the origin of life and the appearance of design in living organisms, mental evidence related to consciousness and free agency, and moral evidence related to transcendent moral truths and obligations.

What do we learn from the Bible itself about how valid and powerful the external, natural (cosmological) evidence for God's existence is? (See Psalm 19:1–4; Romans 1:18–20.)

_____

_____

_____

What do you see as the benefit(s) of investigating and using such evidence in building a case for the truth claims of Christianity?

_____

_____

_____

The idea that evidence unequivocally "says" one thing rather than another is a common misconception that arises when defending the case for theism or Christianity. When evaluating evidence, keep the following in mind:

> Scientific experiments provide us with data. Historic investigations (including criminal investigations) provide us with facts. The raw data and facts don't speak, say, or tell us anything. Observers and thinkers assess the data and facts, interpret them, and provide "findings" and "conclusions."
>
> The problem, of course, is that observers and thinkers (whether they are scientists, historians, or common jurors like you and me) have presuppositional biases that affect the way we form conclusions. If, for example, the evaluator is part of a post-enlightenment scientific community committed to philosophical naturalism (the idea that nothing exists outside the natural realm of the material universe), he or she will find a way to interpret every piece of evidence to confirm his or her naturalistic presuppositions, even if the best inference points to something supernatural.
>
> If, as an evaluator of evidence, you are already committed to a particular answer before you investigate a question, you'll find a way to arrive at the answer you started with.

In what way does understanding this explanation of what evidence "says" help you in presenting the case for Christianity?

_____

_____

In realizing why someone might reject it?

_____

_____

_____

_____

In examining your own assumptions and biases so that you can discern truth from error?

_____

_____

_____

_____

TAKE A PERSONAL ASSESSMENT
(4 MINUTES – EXAMINE YOUR OWN SITUATION AND ANSWER THE QUESTIONS)

If you want to develop a forensic faith, you'll need to become a good investigator. It is a challenging task, but an exciting and rewarding one as well. Like any investigator, you'll need a "kit" with the right tools for the job. Your investigative kit might include a Bible with wide margins in which you can take notes, a notepad for writing down evidence, colored pens for indicating different types of evidence, colored adhesive "tabs" for book marking, and reference books of your choosing, such as a Bible commentary.

What else would you include in your investigative kit?

_____

_____

_____

_____

Which Bible reference tools do you think would be most helpful to your investigation?

_____

_____

_____

_____

Which external sources might you turn to in order to find corroborating evidence for your particular investigation? Consider some of these resources:

The Canon of the New Testament: Its Origin, Development, and Significance
by Bruce Metzger (Oxford University Press, 1997)
The Historical Reliability of the Gospels
by Craig Blomberg (InterVarsity, 2007)
Revisiting the Corruption of the New Testament: Manuscript, Patristic, and Apocryphal Evidence
by Daniel B. Wallace (Kregel, 2011)
Early Manuscripts and Modern Translations of the New Testament
by Philip Comfort (Wipf and Stock, 2001)
Can We Trust the Gospels?: Investigating the Reliability of Matthew, Mark, Luke, and John
by Mark D. Roberts (Crossway, 2007)
The Fathers of the Church, Expanded Edition
by Mike Aquilina (Our Sunday Visitor, November 2006)

What are the best ways for you to organize evidential information—by lists or visual diagrams? By questions or objections? By topic or chronology?

_____

_____

_____

_____

FORM A STRATEGIC PLAN

(5 MINUTES – EXAMINE YOUR CALENDAR AND CREATE AN ACTION PLAN)

Remember the claim you began to investigate after the previous study session? Return to that claim and make a list of the evidence you've uncovered so far. (You could also choose a different claim to investigate if you prefer.)

As you read through your list of evidence, even though it is certainly not complete, you will see your case begin to take shape. Using your list, compose a brief and powerful summary—a recap of the evidence to this point—using no more than 150 words. This summary is, as it presently stands, your case.

_____

_____

_____

_____

_____

_____

_____

_____

Now take the time to test your work and improve your case for that claim. Put it on your calendar. If you want to rehearse by presenting your case to a Christian friend (or friends), who is that friend(s)?

_____

When will you make your practice presentation?

_____

After making your practice presentation, you may need to gather more evidence before you formally (or informally) make the case to someone who is not a believer. But if your evidence is sufficient, move forward to the presentation stage now. (And if you aren't yet ready, don't forget to put a date on your calendar as soon as possible.)

Who is the person(s) to whom you want to present the case for Christianity you have assembled?

_____

When would be a good opportunity for you to present the case to that person?

_____

_____

_____

If you can set a specific date, time, and place to talk with that person, do it. If not, give yourself a specific time frame, perhaps a week or two, during which you are likely to spend time with that person and have an opportunity to share your case: _____

MAKE A CLOSING STATEMENT
(1 MINUTE – CONTEMPLATE AND PRAY)

Building an evidence file for Christian case making is one of the most important things we can do to grow in *our* faith and to become equipped to help other people grow in *their* faith. God has given us more than enough evidence—from His Word, through the world around us, and even from those who oppose Him—to make the case for Christianity. May we always be eager, faithful, and diligent investigators of God's truth.

Dear Lord, thank You for opportunities such as this to learn how we can gather and organize the evidence and become better Christian case makers.

Please guide and encourage us as we consider biblical evidence that answers specific questions about Christianity and supports its claims. May we not feel overwhelmed by the task ahead but excited about the benefits of such an investigation. May our efforts not only strengthen our faith but aid us in communicating to others what we believe and why we believe it. In Jesus's name we pray, amen.

CONDUCT A SECONDARY INVESTIGATION
(60 MINUTES – READ FOR BETTER UNDERSTANDING)

To better understand the issues raised in this session, read the second half of chapter 3 in *Forensic Faith: A Homicide Detective Makes the Case for a More Reasonable, Evidential Christian Faith*, "Intense Investigation: 5 Practices to Help You Examine the Claims of Christianity Like a Good Detective." Read through the last two investigative practices (pages 117 to 146). Take notes specifically for the following section of chapter 3:

Does All This Evidence Really "Say" Anything? (page 142)

_____

_____

_____

_____

_____

_____

_____

_____

_____

Session Six
CONVINCING
COMMUNICATION, PART 1
Select Your "Jurors" Insightfully

Preparing to offer his final remarks, the prosecutor stepped up to the jury box and put his left hand on his waist. He gestured to the jury with his right hand and pointed back in my direction. "When Detective Wallace brings me a case, he has the difficult task of releasing it to me for the trial. All the effort he spent investigating and preparing the case for filing is complete. Now he has to hand the case over to me for the jury trial. I know it is difficult for him; it's hard for him to trust me with his hard work. In fact, I bet he still thinks he could have presented the case better than I did."

The jury laughed. They had listened attentively for six weeks, and I could tell they liked him. By this point in the trial, they understood the work involved in investigating and presenting our case. They were also probably glad the trial was coming to a close.

"It's hard to trust your case to someone else," he continued. "Detective Wallace did everything he could do, and then he had to trust me to do everything I could do. He did his job, and he hoped I would do mine. I know how difficult that was for him, because I am about to trust you in the same way Detective Wallace trusted me. I've worked hard to make the case. I did all I could do. I did my job. Now it's time for you to do everything you can do. It's time for you to do your job."

I've worked with this prosecutor for more than fifteen years, so I've heard him say this, or something like it, many times. It's still powerful every time I hear it because it captures an important truth about persuasive communication. You can spend a great deal of time investigating, preparing, and communicating a truth claim, but in the end you need to be comfortable releasing your argument. You do your job, you present your case, then you must trust your jury to do the right thing.

That's why choosing the jury is so important. In fact, when people ask me at what point in a trial that a case is usually won or lost, I say, "At jury selection." The right jury will make the right decision.

This is true even if you aren't presenting a murder case in the Criminal Courts Building in downtown Los Angeles. It's true for those of us who hope to present the case for Christianity to our "jury" of friends, family, and others. So let's learn some lessons about case making that will help us to approach our case presentation wisely, communicate convincingly, and make the most of our forensic faith.

OPEN THE CASE FILE
(4 MINUTES – CONSIDER AND ANSWER THE QUESTIONS)

If we hope to be successful in making a convincing or persuasive case for anything—whether it's a salesman selling life preservers or a teenager asking to borrow a parent's car—it is wise to consider who our intended audience will be. No matter how good a salesperson you are, you're unlikely to make a fortune selling life preservers in the middle of a desert. And if your parents have just grounded you, you probably won't be successful in asking for the car keys. So what do you think makes success more likely when we present the case for Christ?

_____

_____

When you have presented the case for Christianity in the past, how did you choose the person you presented to, and what was the result?

_____

_____

_____

How might we know in advance which people are likely to be curious and will consider with open minds the evidence we provide?

_____

_____

_____

_____

VIEW THE VIDEO TESTIMONY
(12 MINUTES – TAKE NOTES)

What most determines our success when trying a case?

_____

_____

_____

Pick your "jury" according to the openness continuum

_____

_____

_____

Choose the reasonable middle

_____

_____

_____

Select the reachable three-quarters

_____

_____

_____

CONDUCT A GROUP INVESTIGATION
(23 MINUTES – INVESTIGATE THE ISSUES AND ANSWER THE QUESTIONS)

We tend to think that we have to present the case for Christ to *everyone*. And of course there is a sense in which that is true. God offers salvation to everyone and wants everyone to accept His gift of salvation. However, for reasons beyond our control, not everyone wants to know the case for Christ. Not everyone wants to be on our "jury." So how do we know where to invest our case-making efforts? How do we select people who want to hear, or at least are open to considering, the evidence for Christianity?

_____

_____

_____

_____

Even one juror's character or attitude can make a difference in the outcome of a case. Passion, humility, and open-mindedness are highly desirable while apathy, pride, and inflexible bias can be devastating. What might be the risks or benefits of each of these possible characteristics for potential "jurors" when we are making a case for Christianity?

_____

_____

_____

_____

THE PITFALL OF PRIDE

As our knowledge increases, so can our pride. In Proverbs 16:18, the Bible warns, "Pride goes before destruction, and a haughty spirit before stumbling." It's an important warning to remember in case making no matter which side you are on.

It can be difficult to share truth with "jurors" who think they have mastered a subject. But they aren't the only ones in jeopardy from arrogance. When a detective takes the stand in a criminal case and comes off as arrogant, his testimony is likely to be rejected by a jury. Likewise, prosecutors and attorneys who appear haughty or self-important typically alienate the very jury they are trying to convince. Christian case makers also place themselves at risk when we allow pride to characterize our efforts.

When pride and arrogance encounter pride and arrogance, nothing good results. Case makers who are humble, self-effacing, and gracious are far more likely to draw out those characteristics in the people they are trying to reach.

What also might be the risks or benefits of these characteristics in those of us who desire to be Christian case makers?

_____

_____

_____

_____

Jesus often spoke to a "pool" of people—sometimes thousands at a time—but He was careful and wise in selecting the audience to whom He would present His case in detail. Carefully read and consider what took place in Luke 5:1–11, when Jesus separated a few fishermen from the rest of the crowd. Which characteristics of good "jurors" do you think Jesus might have seen in these men?

_____

_____

_____

_____

When Jesus provided evidence of who He was through the miracle of an excessively abundant catch, how did they respond?

_____

_____

_____

What does their response demonstrate about their suitability as "jurors"?

_____

_____

_____

_____

 Just as the prosecution and defense evaluate potential jurors to determine their bias and suitability as jurors, Christian case makers benefit greatly by choosing the most suitable "jurors," or hearers. Discuss the various positions on the openness continuum diagram so that you understand the three-quarters principle.

_____

_____

_____

_____

What insight does the three-quarters principle shed on the outcomes of your past experiences in sharing your faith?

_____

_____

_____

What potential benefits do you see in applying the three-quarters principle to the process of choosing the individuals with whom you will share your faith in the future?

_____

_____

_____

 Now it's your turn to practice assessing some "jurors" for Christian case making. Read each of the Bible passages below and see which good (or bad) juror qualities you recognize, and do your best to identify where each potential juror falls on the openness continuum.

New Testament Jury Pool: Potential Juror Assessment Chart

Bible Passage	Potential "Juror(s)"	Characteristics Pro and Con	Openness Position
Mark 7:24–30	Woman		
John 1:35–51	John		
	John's disciples		
	Simon Peter		
	Philip		
	Nathanael		
Acts 8:26–39	Philip		
	Ethiopian		
Acts 19:23–29	Demetrius		
	Ephesian craftsmen		

What did Jesus do before He selected His "jury"? How does His example inform our preparation for choosing the right hearers for our case making? (See Luke 6:12–16.)

_____

_____

_____

TAKE A PERSONAL ASSESSMENT
(4 MINUTES – EXAMINE YOUR OWN SITUATION AND ANSWER THE QUESTIONS)

As you did this study, perhaps you thought of people—potential "jurors"—for whom you would like to present the case for Christianity. Who are they? Make a list of all the people you'd like to reach with the case for Christianity:

Name	Openness Position
_____	_____
_____	_____
_____	_____
_____	_____

Who needs to be convinced of the importance of a forensic faith?

_____

_____

Who is struggling with their Christian belief and needs a stronger, evidential foundation?

_____

_____

Who is seeking answers as an atheist or agnostic and needs to be exposed to powerful evidence for God?

_____

_____

 Who is in adamant spiritual rebellion and simply needs prayer?

_____

_____

 ## FORM A STRATEGIC PLAN
(5 MINUTES – EXAMINE YOUR CALENDAR AND CREATE AN ACTION PLAN)

Every trial is set to begin on a predetermined date. Setting a date is important for Christian case makers too. We must decide what kind of case we will present, and we need to set aside time to prepare our case so that we can present it to the best of our ability. So, put your case-making plan on paper.

Which case-for-the-truth claims of Christianity do you want to present?

_____

_____

How long will you allow yourself to prepare this case?_____

Write down your list of potential "jurors" (from your personal assessment above), and identify a position (group 1–4) on the openness continuum for each. Then write out a plan of action for each person. For example, your action plan for a person in group #4 may be to pray for that person to become more open. A person in group #2 or #3 may be the person you select as your primary juror for whom you will prepare to present your case.

Juror's Name	Group #	My Plan of Action
_____	_____	_____
		_____
_____	_____	_____
		_____
		_____
_____	_____	_____
		_____
_____	_____	_____
		_____

Set a date for presenting your case: On _____ I will present my opening

argument to _____.

MAKE A CLOSING STATEMENT
(1 MINUTE – CONTEMPLATE AND PRAY)

Some people have deeply entrenched biases and are hostile toward Christianity, or have had bad experiences with Christians. Although it may be unwise for us to set our sights on people such as these to be the *primary* focus of our Christian case-making efforts, we must remember our responsibility to be loving, compassionate, and consistent ambassadors of Jesus Christ.

Dear Lord, we thank You for Your presence with us, for always watching over us and loving us. We desire to do the right things that will help to overcome the negative perceptions some people have of Christians, Christianity, and You. Please guide us in influencing non-Christians positively without compromising our role as Your ambassadors. We want to make You proud. May we be more sensitive and

responsive to what's really keeping people who reject You from recognizing and responding positively to Your truth. In the precious name of Jesus we pray, amen.

CONDUCT A SECONDARY INVESTIGATION
(60 MINUTES – READ FOR BETTER UNDERSTANDING)

To better understand the issues raised in this session, read the first part of chapter 4 in *Forensic Faith: A Homicide Detective Makes the Case for a More Reasonable, Evidential Christian Faith*, "Convincing Communication: 5 Principles to Help You Share What You Believe Like a Good Prosecutor." Read through the first forensic faith principle (pages 147 to 162). Take notes specifically for the following sections of chapter 4:

Good Jurors Are Passionate Jurors (page 150)

_____

_____

_____

_____

_____

_____

_____

Good Jurors Are Unbiased Jurors (page 151)

_____

_____

_____

_____

_____

_____

_____

Good Jurors Are Humble Jurors (page 153)

_____

_____

_____

_____

_____

_____

_____

_____

Session Seven

CONVINCING
COMMUNICATION, PART 2

Instruct Your "Jury" Evidentially

Jesus carefully selected twelve men to be His first disciples and instructed them specifically so that they could perform their mission well. When the crowds of people Jesus taught had difficulty understanding His parables, Jesus took His disciples aside and gave them special instruction in order to help them comprehend the meaning of each story and analogy (Matthew 13:1–51). Prior to sending His disciples out to share what they had learned, Jesus instructed them specifically in the manner in which they should travel, engage nonbelievers, and discuss the truth (Matthew 10:1–23).

This is similar to the manner in which jurors are instructed in criminal trials. I've been present during many jury-selection sessions and have realized that during the jury-selection process not only do attorneys learn a lot about jurors, but jurors learn a lot about the nature of evidence and its use in assessing truth claims. Attorneys question potential jurors about what they know related to certain aspects of evidence, and this questioning often serves as a form of instruction.

As evidence is presented at trial and attorneys make their closing arguments, jurors become familiar, either directly or indirectly, with the basic rules of evidence and the nature of good case making. As jurors are released to deliberate on what they've seen and heard, the judge provides specific directions to help them evaluate the evidence. Every state has jury instructions that are part of the criminal code.

Criminal-case jurors benefit greatly from this instruction. However, they aren't the only evaluators who need to be taught about the nature and role of evidence. People who hear the case for Christianity also benefit from evidential instruction. Atheist author Richard Dawkins once wrote:

> *Many of us saw religion as harmless nonsense. Beliefs might lack all supporting evidence but, we thought, if people needed a crutch for consolation, where's the harm? September 11th changed all that.*[3]

People who claim that Christianity (or theistic beliefs in general) "lack all supporting evidence" either aren't familiar with the large body of evidence related to Christianity or aren't familiar with what qualifies as evidence in the first place. If we hope to offer persuasive evidence, we need to educate ourselves as well as our potential "jurors" about the nature and role of evidence in making the case for Christian truth.

OPEN THE CASE FILE
(5 MINUTES - CONSIDER AND ANSWER THE QUESTIONS)

Suppose you order the greatest Christmas gift ever for your child. The gift arrives in a big box emblazoned with the words "Some assembly required." You eagerly open the box and discover what looks like a million pieces. In order for the gift to work, each piece has to be assembled in the proper order and position. As you consider how to put that gift together, which is more important—the pieces or the instruction manual? Why?

_____

_____

 What does an instruction manual help us do with an abundance of pieces?

_____

_____

How does this example help us to better understand the importance of instructing a jury regarding case-making evidence?

_____

_____

_____

_____

VIEW THE VIDEO TESTIMONY
(12 MINUTES – TAKE NOTES)

Instruct the jury about evidence

_____

_____

_____

The ability to make a case doesn't mean the case is true

_____

_____

_____

Everything has the potential to be assessed as evidence

_____

_____

_____

Whoever makes the claim bears the burden of proof

_____

_____

_____

Reasonable matters; possible doesn't

_____

_____

_____

The more cumulative the evidence, the stronger the case

_____

_____

_____

Consider witnesses reliable unless demonstrated otherwise

_____

_____

_____

CONDUCT A GROUP INVESTIGATION
(23 MINUTES – INVESTIGATE THE ISSUES AND ANSWER THE QUESTIONS)

When skeptics say the case for Christianity is weak because it can't be built with scientific, testable, physical, forensic evidence, they simply don't know how criminal cases are tried every day in America. Evidence can be divided into two broad categories: *direct* and *indirect*. Direct evidence is simply the *testimony of eyewitnesses*. Indirect evidence (also called "circumstantial evidence") is *everything else*. And everything else is *a lot*.

We need to help people understand that just about everything has the potential to be an important piece of evidence. A detective investigating a particular suspect may consider eyewitness statements and the testimony of those who listened to the statements of these witnesses, behaviors observed on the part of the suspect and the witnesses, material evidence at the scene (including biological and physical evidence), corroborative evidence of all types, the deficiency of evidence or alternative explanations, and statements made (or omitted) by the person being investigated. These types of evidence are used to prosecute criminal trials every day. So, let's consider how the rules of evidence apply in Christian case making:

Don't Assume Something Is True Just Because Someone with Authority Says It, Suggests It, or Makes a Case for It

What has been your experience when someone with authority makes a bold case for a view that is hostile to the claims of Christianity, and what impact did the experience have on you?

_____

_____

_____

How prepared were you at the time to evaluate that person's evidence and respond with an appropriate presentation of evidence for the truth claims of Christianity?

_____

_____

_____

_____

_____

_____

IS IT EVIDENCE?

Nothing that the attorneys say is evidence. In their opening statements and closing arguments, the attorneys will discuss the case, but their remarks are not evidence. Their questions are not evidence. Only the witnesses' answers are evidence. The attorneys' questions are significant only if they help you understand the witnesses' answers. Do not assume that something is true just because one of the attorneys asks a question that suggests it is true.

How might you handle the situation differently today, and what might still be a struggle for you?

_____

_____

_____

Everything Has Evidential Value

What are some good ways to respond to a person who claims that your evidence for Christianity isn't "real" evidence?

_____

_____

_____

_____

Whoever Makes the Claim Bears the Burden of Proof

When there is evidence that demands an explanation, everyone who offers a potential cause or explanation for the evidence bears the burden of proof. But when it comes to discussion about the nature of the universe and the existence of God, Christians typically are in the one-sided position of having to defend their beliefs. Why don't we expect (or even require) both positions to share an equal evidential burden?

_____

_____

_____

_____

What would be a good way to broaden the discussion and ask those who deny the existence of God how they account for a universe without God?

_____

_____

_____

_____

Possibilities Are Irrelevant

The standard of proof for criminal trials is "beyond a reasonable doubt," not "beyond a possible doubt." It's the juror's responsibility to determine the most reasonable inference from evidence, in spite of whatever imaginary or possible doubts he or she might have. What would be your approach if you were presenting the case for Christianity to a skeptic who embraces naturalistic theories about the origin of the universe yet insists on a case for God's existence that is free of any possible doubts?

_____

_____

_____

_____

The More Cumulative the Case, the More Reasonable the Conclusion

What makes cumulative cases effective ways to demonstrate that a claim is true?

_____

_____

_____

_____

Witnesses Are Reliable Unless Demonstrated Otherwise

The surprising truth about reliable witnesses is that they seldom ever agree, their testimony may raise additional questions, and they may actually be incorrect in some details. In what ways does this standard for what makes a reliable witness differ from what you thought?

_____

_____

_____

_____

When might it be helpful to raise the point about what makes a reliable witness when you are presenting the case for Christian truth claims?

_____

_____

_____

It is one thing to instruct a jury about evaluating evidence. After all, a jury is a captive audience. But it is not as easy to instruct the people to whom we present our case about how to think about evidence. What might be some ways you could incorporate evidential instruction into your case presentation?

_____

_____

_____

Which questions might you ask to determine your hearer's understanding of or expectations about evidence?

_____

_____

_____

TAKE A PERSONAL ASSESSMENT
(4 MINUTES – EXAMINE YOUR OWN SITUATION AND ANSWER THE QUESTIONS)

When you think about it, all of us have experience as cumulative case makers. For example, how often do we give more than one reason when we are asked certain questions? If one of your coworkers asked you why you chose the particular model of car you bought, are you likely to say simply, "I liked the color," or are you more inclined to say, "I liked the styling, but what is under the hood really got my attention. I like the feel I have behind the wheel, and you ought to see how it performs on the open road"? The latter explanation may be brief, but it is a cumulative argument.

To boost your case-making abilities, build a six-point cumulative case right now about choices, events, or household practices that are common in everyday life. You might build a case for why a certain breed of dog or cat is good to own, why family holiday traditions are important, or why your favorite sports team will make the playoffs.

Your Claim:

_____

Your Cumulative Case:

1. _____
2. _____
3. _____
4. _____
5. _____
6. _____
7. _____

Keep practicing this exercise for different things you encounter in daily life. When we realize how often we build cumulative cases in our lives, it's not as intimidating to build a cumulative case for the truth claims of Christianity.

 ### FORM A STRATEGIC PLAN
(5 MINUTES – EXAMINE YOUR CALENDAR AND CREATE AN ACTION PLAN)

Many Christians are not prepared for the current hostility some people express toward believers and the claims of Christianity. But if we're going to present the case for Christ, we cannot isolate ourselves from different viewpoints. We need to know and prepare for what we might face.

One way to sample the arguments and disposition of people with opposing views is to join an atheist group on a social media platform. You can join such groups without having to engage with the content (in fact, it's unwise to comment or converse in such settings until you are confident in your case-making abilities), and you'll learn a lot by "listening in" to what is being discussed by others.

Beyond gathering information, there's no substitute for *practice*. We need to become adept at discovering the views of our potential "jurors" regarding evidence. We need to practice different ways we might instruct them in the validity and application of evidence. Finally, we need to make sure we are prepared to defend the reliability of our evidence if it is attacked. One of the best ways to do this is to *role play*.

Who is a like-minded Christian case maker with whom you could practice these skills?

_____

Call that person now. Set a date, _____, and begin challenging each other to be proficient case makers for the most important case the world has ever known.

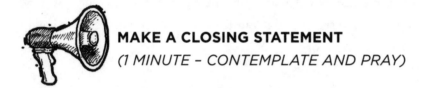

MAKE A CLOSING STATEMENT
(1 MINUTE – CONTEMPLATE AND PRAY)

Knowing the evidence and how to assemble it is essential if we are to be effective witnesses for Christ. It is also necessary for us to learn how to instruct our "jurors," the people to whom we present our case, so that they understand the role evidence plays in the case for Christianity.

Dear Lord, we come before You grateful that You are the God of truth. We thank You that You are reliable, trustworthy, and faithful in all You do. Help us discern truth from error as we gather evidence and build a case we can communicate to others. Be with us and guide us when we present the case for Christianity to people who may reject You. May we never be shaken just because others are vocal in making their case against You. Instead, may we be encouraged to keep building the case so that it becomes stronger and more convincing. In Jesus's name we pray, amen.

CONDUCT A SECONDARY INVESTIGATION
(60 MINUTES – READ FOR BETTER UNDERSTANDING)

To better understand the issues raised in this session, read the second part of chapter 4 in *Forensic Faith: A Homicide Detective Makes the Case for a More Reasonable, Evidential Christian Faith*, "Convincing Communication: 5 Principles to Help You Share What You Believe Like a Good Prosecutor." Read through forensic faith principle 2 (pages 162 to 176). Take notes specifically for the following sections of chapter 4:

Reliable Eyewitnesses Seldom Appear to Agree (page 174)

_____

_____

_____

_____

_____

_____

_____

Reliable Eyewitnesses Raise Questions (page 175)

_____

_____

_____

_____

_____

_____

_____

Reliable Eyewitnesses Are Sometimes Incorrect (page 175)

_____

_____

_____

_____

_____

_____

_____

_____

Session Eight

CONVINCING COMMUNICATION, PART 3

Present Your Case with Confidence

I'll never forget a case I had many years ago involving a new district attorney during his first year of trying felony cases. He was exceptionally bright and articulate. During preparation for the trial, I grew increasingly excited about what this young attorney might do in front of a jury. My expectations were crushed, however, once he stepped behind the podium and began his opening statement.

It's one thing to be intellectually capable or academically prepared, but it's another to confidently and enthusiastically deliver what you've prepared to an audience. My young attorney colleague can attest to the struggle many people have when trying to communicate what they believe to others, especially during the opening minutes. On the other hand, my good friend Deputy District Attorney John Lewin is perhaps the finest communicator I know. Although he wasn't always a confident, enthusiastic speaker, John has mastered the art of first impressions. His enthusiastic opening statements garner immediate respect and attention from the jury.

When Jesus spoke, His "opening statements" were the best ever delivered. No one quite captured the attention and imagination of an audience like Jesus did. His followers were inspired even as His adversaries were challenged and convicted. Consider, for example, how Jesus began a conversation with His disciples about their future:

> *See to it that no one misleads you. Many will come in My name, saying, "I am He!" and will mislead many. When you hear of wars and rumors of wars, do not be frightened; those things must take place; but that is not yet the end.*

For nation will rise up against nation, and kingdom against kingdom; there
will be earthquakes in various places; there will also be famines. These things
are merely the beginning of birth pangs. (Mark 13:5–8)

How could that opening statement not capture the attention of Jesus's disciples and have them poised, eager, and waiting for more?

As a Christian case maker, I don't expect to craft my opening statements as well as Jesus did. It's often intimidating to initiate spiritual conversations that allow us to present the case for Christ. But I am eager to do my best. I want to make a good first impression and present the case with confidence, clarity, and conviction. In the end, I want my hearers to become Christ followers who someday make the case to others.

OPEN THE CASE FILE
(4 MINUTES – CONSIDER AND ANSWER THE
QUESTIONS)

For many of us, public speaking is a challenge—regardless if we are the speaker or the listener. Most of us can remember hearing speeches that couldn't end soon enough. We can also remember speeches that we could have enjoyed for longer. What's the best persuasive speech you have ever heard, and what made it meaningful and memorable for you?

_____

_____

_____

How significant was the opening of that speech to your overall experience, and how would you characterize it?

_____

_____

VIEW THE VIDEO TESTIMONY
(13 MINUTES – TAKE NOTES)

Make your opening statement with great enthusiasm

_____

_____

Keep your audience engaged

_____

_____

_____

Preparation and practice

_____

_____

Make good on your promises

_____

_____

_____

Make your presentation accessible

_____

_____

Close your argument with confidence

_____

_____

_____

CONDUCT A GROUP INVESTIGATION

(23 MINUTES – INVESTIGATE THE ISSUES AND ANSWER THE QUESTIONS)

No matter how well we research and organize the evidence for Christianity, we must be prepared to deliver the case well if we hope to have a life-changing impact. Let's consider some of the strategic decisions and practices that allow us to communicate a case with conviction and confidence:

 Opening statements are vital to a successful trial outcome. If you can convince the jury early, all you have to do is keep up the momentum. If you don't convince them early, you will be playing catch-up for the rest of the trial. What do you think is necessary to make an impressive opening statement, and why?

_____

_____

_____

_____

 Grover Peterson is eager and courageous when starting spiritual conversations because he has prepared a simple, engaging, and inoffensive opening statement. When he approaches people, he usually points out something—perhaps a watch or a pen—in their immediate environment that is clearly designed for a specific purpose. He then will ask, "Everything in life has a design, function, and purpose. What is yours?" What does his approach demonstrate that can help you make a more effective opening statement?

_____

_____

_____

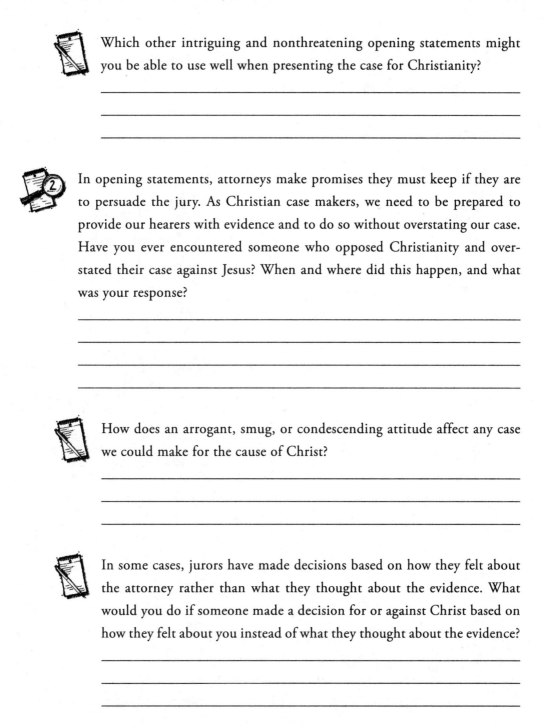

Which other intriguing and nonthreatening opening statements might you be able to use well when presenting the case for Christianity?

_____

_____

_____

In opening statements, attorneys make promises they must keep if they are to persuade the jury. As Christian case makers, we need to be prepared to provide our hearers with evidence and to do so without overstating our case. Have you ever encountered someone who opposed Christianity and overstated their case against Jesus? When and where did this happen, and what was your response?

_____

_____

_____

_____

How does an arrogant, smug, or condescending attitude affect any case we could make for the cause of Christ?

_____

_____

_____

In some cases, jurors have made decisions based on how they felt about the attorney rather than what they thought about the evidence. What would you do if someone made a decision for or against Christ based on how they felt about you instead of what they thought about the evidence?

_____

_____

_____

We can count on our hearers to fact check everything we say, so we need to be prepared to back up our claims with accurate evidence. How do you respond when someone doubts or questions what you say?

_____

_____

_____

What ideas might you share for remaining gracious, respectful, and confident when our instinct may be to feel insecure or threatened?

_____

_____

_____

_____

_____

_____

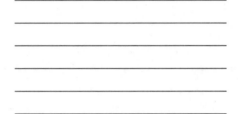

PRACTICE BEFORE YOU PRESENT

Long before I ever began making the case for Christianity publicly, I worked diligently to refine my presentation skills. I spent many hours at my dinner table practicing the case with a close friend who was my harshest and most affirming critic. I also spent hours in the car by myself listening to recordings of presentations and debates by accomplished Christian apologists. I would then practice repeating or responding to their cases. The more we practice, talk, and teach, the better we will be when we present our case to others.

In addition to knowing our claims and our evidence well, how can we gain experience in presenting that evidence to others, especially to those who may be very hostile to Christianity?

_____

_____

_____

Good communicators avoid confusing, esoteric, technical, or proprietary language. To use a baseball analogy, good communicators "throw the ball so people can catch it." Unfortunately, some of the words, phrases, or images that Christians often use to speak about their faith may confuse or even offend people who are not believers. We need to listen carefully to the words we use and learn to translate our "Christian language" into a more accessible version of our native tongue. Before you became a Christian, which phrases or words didn't make sense to you or made it difficult to understand the truth about Christianity?

_____

_____

_____

As a group, make a list of some of the troublesome words or phrases and translate them into more accessible terms.

Christian Term: **Translation Expression:**

_____   _____

_____   _____

_____   _____

_____   _____

_____   _____

_____   _____

Good communicators also ask good questions. Our objective in Christian case making is not to steamroll over our hearers but to capture their attention and address their spiritual questions with the truth of Christianity. Greg Koukl, author of *Tactics: A Game Plan for Discussing Your Christian Convictions*, suggests asking two important questions when someone makes a claim about Christianity or God: "What do you mean by that?" and "Why do you think that's true?" What might you learn from a person's answers to these simple questions that would help you present a stronger case?

_____

_____

_____

What other questions could you ask to clarify what a person believes, and why?

_____

_____

A closing argument is an impassioned plea for the jury to remember what they've heard and seen and to make the right decision. It is an opportunity to leave people with a final memorable statement. Jesus was an expert at delivering a good closing argument. Read the argument He presented in Matthew 7:24–29. What decision or action did Jesus call His hearers to make?

_____

_____

_____

Which words would you use to describe His presentation, and what impact did it have on those who heard Him?

_____

_____

_____

Jesus knew He wouldn't be the last person to make a case for Christianity. Who has the responsibility for making the case for Christianity today? (See Matthew 28:18–20.)

_____

_____

_____

On what basis, then, can each of us be powerful and confident case makers?

_____

_____

_____

TAKE A PERSONAL ASSESSMENT
(4 MINUTES – EXAMINE YOUR OWN SITUATION AND ANSWER THE QUESTIONS)

As we conclude this final group session, how ready and prepared are you to present a case for your Christian beliefs? _____

What work do you still need to do to prepare your evidence?

_____

_____

_____

Identify any areas of weakness in case making that concern you. What action can you take to be more proficient in each area?

_____

_____

_____

To what extent do you view your case-making conversations as "solo efforts"— and think that the entire outcome depends on you?

_____

_____

_____

In what ways does that view affect your desire and ability to actively engage in making a case for Christianity?

_____

_____

_____

Today, you may not be the confident Christian case maker you would like to be. But don't be discouraged. The disciples weren't the kind of case makers they wanted to be when they first met Jesus either. It takes time to become a good case maker. But by the power of the Holy Spirit, each of us can accept our duty, train to defend the truth, investigate the evidence, and make the case.

You're part of a larger team, powered by the Spirit of God. So be faithful. Keep making the case. You never know which "hit" will be the winning run.

FORM A STRATEGIC PLAN
(5 MINUTES – EXAMINE YOUR CALENDAR AND CREATE AN ACTION PLAN)

It is time for us to get busy together as the church. Now more than ever, it's time for us to accept our duty as case makers and start training. It's time to investigate the case for Christianity and communicate it convincingly to others. It's time for all of us to become "sheepdogs" who protect and serve the "sheep."

Time is short. Those of us who understand our duty as Christian case makers need to help others see their duty as well. Although there are many incredibly valuable apologists in the Christian community, we need many more to rise up and protect the sheep from the wolves who would draw them away from Christ, the Good Shepherd.

You don't have to be the biggest (or strongest) sheepdog in the field to make a difference. But you do have to act. There's just one pivotal question left: How willing are you to get in the "game" of Christian case making? To become a sheepdog who guards against those who present seemingly strong arguments against God and Christian beliefs? If you are willing, what will you do to encourage other people to learn what you've learned during this session?

_____

_____

_____

Who can you recruit to stand with you in being a "sheepdog"?

_____

_____

_____

_____

_____

Set a date (or an occasion) to make it happen. _____

MAKE A CLOSING STATEMENT
(1 MINUTE – CONTEMPLATE AND PRAY)

When we are willing to accept and embrace our Christian duty as case makers, we'll change the trajectory of the lives around us and grow in confidence as followers of Jesus. May what we've learned through this series of studies ignite in us a desire to change the way we think about sharing the truth claims of Christianity and encourage us to engage in bold, competent, and practiced case making. May each of us remain on a lifelong investigative journey, learning to love Jesus with all our mind as well as all our heart and soul.

Dear Lord, we thank You for Your sacrificial death and resurrection that save us from our sins and preserve for us an eternity in heaven with You. We are privileged that You have chosen us to be Your disciples, Your ambassadors to the world. Kindle within us the urgency and passion to be effective case makers. Help us to remember that despite our struggles and mistakes, You are with us. May Your Spirit teach us through our errors and encourage us to continue taking incremental steps toward becoming the best Christian case makers we can be. Thank You for the opportunities we have, and will have in the future, to "get in the game," make the case, and "guard the sheep." In Jesus's name we pray, amen.

CONDUCT A SECONDARY INVESTIGATION
(60 MINUTES – READ FOR BETTER UNDERSTANDING)

To better understand the issues raised in this session, read the last part of chapter 4 in *Forensic Faith: A Homicide Detective Makes the Case for a More Reasonable, Evidential Christian Faith*, "Convincing Communication: 5 Principles to Help You Share What You Believe Like a Good Prosecutor." Read through forensic faith principles 3–5 (pages 176 to 200). Also, read the postscript: "Become a Sheepdog" (page 201). Take notes specifically for the following section of the postscript:

The Importance of Sheepdogs (page 202)

_____

_____

_____

_____

_____

_____

_____

Discover Your Readiness in 21 Minutes

The Forensic Faith Readiness Review is a simple seven-question survey. It's downloadable from our website as a printable PDF file,[4] and it's designed to evaluate your strengths and weaknesses as a Christian case maker. If you don't have access to the website or a printer, you can still evaluate yourself in the following manner:

1. Start with seven lined pieces of notebook paper.

2. Write the following questions at the top of each page (one per page). These questions are designed to reflect the most common questions and objections offered by skeptics:

a. Why are you a Christian (be honest about this response, in spite of what we've already discussed in session 1 of this guide)?

b. What evidence do you have to believe God exists?

c. Why do you trust what the Bible says about Jesus?

d. Why would God send people to hell just because they don't believe in Jesus?

e. If God is all-loving and all-powerful, why is there so much evil in the world?

f. If God is the creator of everything, who created God?

g. Why would a loving God command the total destruction of all of Israel's enemies (including their children and livestock)?

3. Take three minutes to answer each question before moving on to the next page. Set a timer and do your best to respect these time limits. The entire review should take only twenty-one minutes. Remember, in a real conversation, you may not get much more time than this review allows.

4. After answering the questions, make your own assessment about the answers you've given. Be honest with yourself. Was it difficult to think of a response for each question? Did you struggle to articulate an answer without simply relying on your own subjective experience? While there aren't necessarily "right" or "wrong" answers for each question, some responses are definitely more persuasive than others. Do you think unbelievers would be satisfied with *your* answers, especially if they asked for objective evidence to support your claims? For a point of comparison, you can refer to the articles linked in the Forensic Faith Readiness Review at ForensicFaithBook.com. (You can also find a set of these article links in the Evidence Locker Section at the end of *Forensic Faith: A Homicide Detective Makes the Case for a More Reasonable, Evidential Christian Faith*.)

If you're a parent, you can give an abbreviated version of this test to your own children. We've arranged these questions in order of difficulty. Older students are certainly capable of completing the review just as it is written, but you can shorten the number of questions to suit your own situation. If you think your elementary-aged students are up to it, you might ask them to answer the first three questions, for example, allowing five minutes for each answer. Better yet, ask these questions in an informal way during your next dinner conversation or trip in the car.

This brief Readiness Review will likely open your eyes to your own competency and to the readiness of the young people in your family. Don't be discouraged if you have difficulty answering the questions or are unhappy with the quality of your responses. That's the whole purpose of the review: to form a starting point from which you can begin to grow and improve. These are the kinds of questions skeptics ask and the kinds of questions young Christians struggle to answer. Many young people, when asked why they left the church in their college years, cited the difficulty they had in finding someone in their Christian community or family who could adequately answer similar objections.[5] We need to prepare ourselves with the answers. If we want to grow as believers and make a difference in the lives of young Christians, we need to stop *teaching* and start *training*. It all starts with a test.

NOTES

1. For more information about the inarticulate nature of young Christians, please refer to Christian Smith and Melinda Lundquist Denton, *Soul Searching: The Religious and Spiritual Lives of American Teenagers* (Oxford: Oxford University Press, April 13, 2009).

2. Excerpted from Andrew's longer message with his permission.

3. Richard Dawkins, "Has the World Changed?," *Guardian*, October 11, 2001.

4. Visit www.ForensicFaithBook.com to download the assessment test.

5. For more information about this, refer to Smith and Denton, *Soul Searching*.

THE MOST IMPORTANT CASE OF YOUR LIFE

Through the *Forensic Faith Curriculum Kit,* cold-case homicide detective **J. Warner Wallace** shows us why it's important to develop a forensic faith and how to become effective Christian case makers.

This eight-week program will help you
- understand why we have a duty to defend the truth;
- develop a training strategy to master the evidence for Christianity;
- learn how to employ the techniques of a detective to discover new insights from God's Word; and
- become better communicators by learning the skills of professional case makers.

Using real-life detective stories, fascinating strategies, biblical insights, and his own visual illustrations, Wallace shares cold-case investigative disciplines we can apply to our Christian faith.

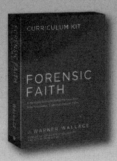
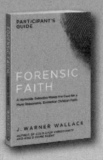

Available in print and digital editions
everywhere books are sold

David C Cook

transforming lives together